Love's Lies

and

Other Deceptions

Title: Love's Lies and Other Deceptions
Author: Mukesh Chhajer
Language: English

Publisher: Mukesh Chhajer
Published: August 2013

Books by Mukesh Chhajer:
- Random Reflections (2006)
- On Life and Liberation: Essays on Jain Practices and Philosophy (2007)
- Silent Voices (2008, 2012)
- समय के रंग (Samay Ke Rang (in Hindi)) (2010, 2012)
- Tirthankar Mahaveer: A Biography in Verse (2010, 2012)
- Momentary Madness (2012)
- Love's Lies and Other Deceptions (2013)

Cover Design: Mukesh Chhajer

Copyright © 2013 Mukesh Chhajer
All rights reserved. No part of this book can be reproduced in any form without the prior written permission of the author.

ISBN-13: 978-0615861685
ISBN-10: 0615861687

Love's Lies
and
Other Deceptions

A collection of poems
by

Mukesh Chhajer

Love's Lies -- Mukesh Chhajer

Love arrives, on the wings of fire
To avoid burns, is not an option
Will the heat burn away the dross
Or only ashes are in the future

Love's Lies -- Mukesh Chhajer

Love does not torture
Beloved does
In this game though
No one loses

***

Beloved does not torture
Love does
In the end though
It is immaterial

Love's Lies -- Mukesh Chhajer

Love got entangled in, worldly affairs
Robbed, bankrupted, kidnapped
It found itself incarcerated
In the heart of man

Restless love, eager to continue its journey
Is forced to compromise
Creating man with broken hearts
And broken minds

Love's Lies -- Mukesh Chhajer

Love is like a river that must
Find a way to flow
Everything that becomes its part
Eventually, becomes pure

Love's Lies -- Mukesh Chhajer

My arms are open, to welcome the beloved
But the beloved has decided, to wait

To test my patience and resolve
Throwing my way, a few enticing offers

A cruel play, how can though I say
It's unfair, the beloved only accepts

What is pure and unblemished
I only hope, I would still have something

To offer, when the game ends

Love's Lies -- Mukesh Chhajer

Love got defeated, in a battle of one-upmanship
Delighted with outcome, it engaged in another
Then another and another, until it lost all
To earn the highest honor

Love's Lies -- Mukesh Chhajer

Love can never be given
Love can never be demanded
Love can never be extracted
Love can never be acquired

Love just overflows, suddenly
When you have become, helpless
To immerse anyone who comes
Within the circle, of its influence

Love's Lies -- Mukesh Chhajer

Love explodes when least expected
To soak in bliss, body-and-soul
Few though have, the courage to venture
Fewer even, willing to endure

In a world, where possession is supreme
The purest of all, wanders without home

Love's Lies -- Mukesh Chhajer

Love arrived, in the most innocuous way
But I was too busy, decorating house
Engaged in debates and, winning arguments
Losing the opportunity, to savor its sweetness

Love's Lies -- Mukesh Chhajer

Love gets trampled, under the tiniest feet
Love can withstand, the weight of a mountain
Love is neither weak, nor strong
It is a river that knows, how
To reach its destination

Love's Lies -- Mukesh Chhajer

Love never begs
Love never demands
Love merely observes
The unfolding of its own fragrance

Love's Lies -- Mukesh Chhajer

Love was free, God's gift
To its beloved creation
It became a tool, in the hands
Of God's most advanced creature

A gift to be shared and enjoyed
Love has become a commodity
Traded on a market place
Wrapped in attractive packages
For the right price

Suffocated, love seeks escape
Leaving behind an empty heart
And empty bottles of
Vodka, rum and gin

Love's Lies -- Mukesh Chhajer

Every church is afraid
It may lose its congregation

Every temple is afraid
It may lose its visitors

Every mosque, every synagogue lives
In a constant fear of losing its crowd

Except a heart where, even two
Is a sign of an unfaithful love

Love's Lies -- Mukesh Chhajer

The crescent moon has come
Once again, to decapitate
Would you let it or let
This opportunity also, slip away

Preface

Love is a subject as old as humanity itself. Countless volumes have been written on love; classifying, categorizing, analyzing and dissecting it. And yet, love remains as incomprehensible as ever.

Prior to the summer of 2011, I had no desire to write on the subject of love. Until then, I had written only an occasional poem on love. However, during the summer of 2011 I had a chance to read a book, titled "love, freedom, aloneness" by Osho. I found Osho's definition and analysis of love to be very thought provoking. It instigated in me a desire to write on love; a love that is pure and unblemished; a love that is serene yet mischievous, unyielding yet fluid, uncompromising yet caring, exacting yet joyous. The collection of poems presented here is the result. These poems are presented in the chronological order they were written. It is my hope that readers will enjoy these poems as much as I have enjoyed writing them.

Danville VA   Mukesh Chhajer
August 8, 2013

Love's Lies -- Mukesh Chhajer

One word, one thought, one glance
Through the most minor of the moments
Love can enter when least expected
To occupy the center stage

Its influence, thereafter can
Never be fully comprehended
Occupying every thought
Coloring every action
Infused in every breath
It becomes life's, sole purpose

If love is real, otherwise
Every season produces its
Own excitement

Love's Lies -- Mukesh Chhajer

In my surrender, there was
A pinch of arrogance
I got up, licking
A mouthful of dust

Love's Lies -- Mukesh Chhajer

Love never asks, what
Will I get in return
Love-like though run around
With a broken begging bowl

Love's Lies -- Mukesh Chhajer

Love qualified is selfishness
In disguise
Love qualified is insulting
To human life
Love qualified is a business
Of the lowest kind
Love qualified is a disgrace
To the divine

Love's Lies -- Mukesh Chhajer

In love, there is no force
Like water, it enters every pore
Nourishing, without overwhelming
Warm, without scalding
Every moment is a moment of discovery

Love's Lies -- Mukesh Chhajer

Love stood still but I
Was too restless

I stood still but love
Could not decide

Now we both circle around
A void created by
Empty hearts

Love's Lies -- Mukesh Chhajer

Love's promises are always dangerous
Outcomes are perpetually in suspense
The good and the bad, the metric of the world
Invariably loses, its meaning

Cruel is caring, supporting suffocating
Critical is kind, annoying endearing
To judge it by words, devoid of the context
Is to remain unaware, of its true nature

Love's Lies -- Mukesh Chhajer

Love's arrow was sharp
Piercing the heart without
Spilling a drop of blood
No witness, no evidence
A perfect crime

The one who dies, does not cry foul
The one who kills, pays the ultimate price
The hunter and the hunt, becoming one
If the love was, true to itself

Love's Lies -- Mukesh Chhajer

On love, there are many treatises
All are useless when confronted
By their most powerful enemy

If the love you profess, oozes
From your every pore
The experience of it will
Make all the treatises a good
Fodder for a bonfire

Love's Lies -- Mukesh Chhajer

To tie something tightly
It must be solid
Love is too fluid
To be caught in a knot

To wander off aimlessly
Anchor must be weak
Love is too strong
To let you go free

To keep one confined
Walls are needed
Love is too porous
To hold you back

To get lost in the forest
Light must be missing
Love is a beacon
That shows the path

Love's Lies -- Mukesh Chhajer

Love always hurts
How can one clean a pot

Without a good scrub
Heal an open wound

Without discomfort
To clarify butter, it

Must be heated well
Let the process continue

Love knows when to stop
And apply the healing balm

Love's Lies -- Mukesh Chhajer

Love never tramples, it may
Though appear ferocious
A lioness protecting its
Own cubs

Love's Lies -- Mukesh Chhajer

I thought, love will
Meet me at the time, destined

I and love kept our side
Of the bargain

Not so though time, sending
Us back on separate paths

Love's Lies -- Mukesh Chhajer

Through the river, one can
Reach the destination
Sometimes turbulent, sometimes serene
The two go hand-in-hand when
Love is the medium

By the river, there are banks
To rest, to relax, to sit in peace
None though exist, by the love
The only option, to be immersed

When it is flooded, river is dangerous
Uprooting, annihilating, disorienting
It is a blissful existence, in the other case
Even the earth and the heaven are
Eager to witness, such an event

Love's Lies -- Mukesh Chhajer

In love, one never loses
The source, once uncorked
Flows, forever

A mighty river, may
Freeze on the surface
The current underneath
Does not subside

Love's Lies -- Mukesh Chhajer

When love beckoned, I
Ran for cover, having

Never been caught in its cross-fire
How could I have known its

Soothing and nourishing, side effects

Love's Lies -- Mukesh Chhajer

When anger rises, many
A cells are burnt to
Produce, noxious gases

When passion rises, many
A cells are burnt to
Produce, a foul smell

When greed rises, many
A cells are burnt to
Produce, poisonous substances

When love rises, many
A cells are burnt to
Produce, a soothing fragrance

Love's Lies -- Mukesh Chhajer

Love and fear, both hold
With one critical difference
Fear holds, never to release
Love attaches wings, to set one free

Love's Lies -- Mukesh Chhajer

Love does not leave a trail behind
It needs nothing, in return

Love's Lies -- Mukesh Chhajer

Love came, not to conquer
But to surrender

We though considered it an assault
On our independent existence

Making a lonely island
Our eternal abode

Love's Lies -- Mukesh Chhajer

Love is not a river
Neither an ocean
Love does not follow
Any set pattern

Its constraints are freedom
Its absence, unwelcome
Love does not conform to
The language of the world

Love's Lies -- Mukesh Chhajer

Love ran away because
It was angry
Its path though, is circular

Love's Lies -- Mukesh Chhajer

Love is a rock, its nature to support
Are you the earth?

Love is water, its nature to flow
Are you the river?

Love is a spark, its nature to purify
Are you the fire?

Love is air, its nature to circulate
Are you the breath?

Love is space, its nature to accommodate
Are you the sky?

Love's Lies -- Mukesh Chhajer

Love takes a leap, not
Knowing if it will find
A solid ground to stand

To verify in advance though
Would have been just
A business transaction

When love rises from within
Don't let reason stand in the way
Reason looks for fog and hurdles
Love fearlessly strides, unconcerned

Love's Lies -- Mukesh Chhajer

Love is like a rain

A drizzle is soothing
A torrent will quickly bring

One to the destination
Even if for a brief moment

It may appear to drown

Love's Lies -- Mukesh Chhajer

In love, disappointments
Are inherent
A river can realize its strength
Only by overcoming hurdles

Love's Lies -- Mukesh Chhajer

Love is biting
Love is soothing
Both are essential to
Heal a wound

Love's Lies -- Mukesh Chhajer

Ego caused schism
Who can bridge
To make one whole again
Let love be unleashed

Love's Lies -- Mukesh Chhajer

A river can only flow, because it does
Not insist that it be, straight and narrow
How can then love survive
Confined within rigid boundaries

Love's Lies -- Mukesh Chhajer

Love does not survive where
There is a selfish desire
Cheap imitations though are
Found at every street corner

Love's Lies -- Mukesh Chhajer

My love would be real if
Tears would turn in to
A bemused smile on
The face of my beloved seeing
My dead body

Love's Lies -- Mukesh Chhajer

If the beloved is far away, you may
Employ a phone, an email or skype
If near, a touch, a word or
A glance may suffice

How do you communicate though
When your every pore is saturated
And yet the distance remains as wide
As the expanse of the universe

Love's Lies -- Mukesh Chhajer

Love is boiling water
Don't be careless
Its touch will scald
Essential to kill germs

Love's Lies -- Mukesh Chhajer

Love is a sharp-edged sword
Slay or be slain, in the end
There can only be one

Love's Lies -- Mukesh Chhajer

In love, no one comes
First or second
Togetherness is
Its essence

Love's Lies -- Mukesh Chhajer

Love is like a river, calm and serene
Continue to float for a slow dissolution
Or attain instant nirvana, by being immersed

Love's Lies -- Mukesh Chhajer

In a war, one has armor and sword
Bare naked heart faces, arrows of love

In a war, relatives and friends are support
All alone when time comes, to face the beloved

In a war, slay as many as you can
Being slain, many-many times, is love's dictate

Love's Lies -- Mukesh Chhajer

Love's path and faint-of-heart
As good a combination as, darkness-and-light
Don't ever put them, side-by-side
Neither may survive, the ensuing turmoil

Love's Lies -- Mukesh Chhajer

Love ain't hard, if you don't demand
Love ain't simple, if you attach conditions
Love ain't rock, love ain't river
Love is a state of, being complete

Love's Lies -- Mukesh Chhajer

Who else but you, put
Me on the noose
And still demand that
I stay alive

Many have tried, only to accept defeat
Many disappeared, before facing consequences
Many have disowned, their own selves
In the hope of finding, another pool to dive

Yet you remain defiant
Unafraid of consequences
Keeping me alive will only
Tie you down

Love's Lies -- Mukesh Chhajer

Love is an ocean
Wide and deep
Don't judge its character
By the surface waves

Love's Lies -- Mukesh Chhajer

Love's lies are sweet and enticing
A dangerous combination of sound-and-sight
To fall prey is to, lose oneself
To not leaves one, empty and dead

Love's Lies -- Mukesh Chhajer

Love's lane is short, lover's long
One goes through fire, other through
A well-cared lawn

Love's Lies -- Mukesh Chhajer

Love, a result of complex
Biochemical reactions
Can hide behind the mask
Of appearing sane

Or insanity becomes a garb
To hide the state of, utter blissfulness

Illogical, irrational, unpredictable
Love only knows, the language of deception

Love's Lies -- Mukesh Chhajer

You took my breath away
I suffer from, smallness of the heart

Love's Lies -- Mukesh Chhajer

Love's path is lit with fire
Every step demands, a new sacrifice
Further you go, lighter you become
You have arrived, when all is aether

Gold is purified, through fire
Iron is cast, through fire
Copper is drawn, through fire
Love is embraced, through fire

Love's Lies -- Mukesh Chhajer

If doors of the heart are left open
A possibility exists, for a great loss
If doors of the heart are kept closed
Losses will be, the only outcome

Love's Lies -- Mukesh Chhajer

In love, bubbles rise
Without creating an upheaval
Rising bubbles otherwise demonstrate
Only their own importance

Love's Lies -- Mukesh Chhajer

In love, boundaries dissolve
A river rushes, to meet the ocean

In love, heart opens
A tree provides, comfort to all

In love, humanity blooms
A flower shares, its fragrance

In love, compassion rises
A mountain races, to embrace the sky

Love's Lies -- Mukesh Chhajer

Love still has to find me
Sometimes, a river has to run
Upstream, before it can
Reach the ocean

Love's Lies -- Mukesh Chhajer

Love is like a fire that
Burns away all impurities
Leaving behind, a nugget of gold
Hidden under a pile of ashes

Love's Lies -- Mukesh Chhajer

How can I show, my face to the beloved
I am ugly, hideous and lack in purity
The beloved though is, generous and forgiving
My futile attempts, amuse it greatly

Filled with passion, I latch on with both hands
It slips away, like water through fingers
With full determination, I pursue the course
Falling repeatedly, like a child on ice

Filled with anger, I strike with vengeance
It spreads fragrance, like flower when crushed
Filled with greed, I tempt it with seduction
It exposes deception, like sunlight in a dark room

With every attempt, rendered unsuccessful
I accept defeat, with humility and humbleness
With a benign smile, to take away my tiredness
The beloved receives me, with dignity and grace

Love's Lies -- Mukesh Chhajer

Love is neither a truth, nor a lie
Love is a twilight where, every silhouette
Is searching, for its own meaning

Love's Lies -- Mukesh Chhajer

Let love suffer, how else
Would one ascertain its true value
A love that has not walked through fire
Accumulates many impurities

Love's Lies -- Mukesh Chhajer

In the eyes of the beloved, remain worthless
Collectors abound for, every piece of trinket

In the presence of the beloved, remain invisible
Duality breeds, only conflicts and discords

To the words of the beloved, accept without doubts
Truth and lies are, in the purview of rationality and logic

To the disapproval of the beloved, accept with grace
Rewards and honors, promote only competition

Love's Lies -- Mukesh Chhajer

What heart has spoken
Mind has yet to comprehend
What mind has stated
Heart does not accept

Without compromise, the conflict
Promises to rage, until the dooms day
Will the one, who can settle this battle
Be kind enough, to intervene

Love's Lies -- Mukesh Chhajer

Love's lanes are narrow
Uneven, filled with blind turns
Love does not demand
Nor issues, ultimatums

Love is fluid, easily adjusts
Love accepts graciously, humiliations and defeats
Neither grand displays, nor dramatic gestures
Love sacrifices, merely for the amusement
Of the beloved

Love's Lies -- Mukesh Chhajer

In love, there is only one
Duality is a sign of
Unripened state

***

In love, fragrance is subtle
Obscene and superficial, otherwise

***

Love kills all that which is unholy
Without making one, self-righteous

***

Love is never strong or weak
Love is just right, under every situation

Love's Lies -- Mukesh Chhajer

Love is a lie, yet essential
How would a Taj Mahal otherwise
Be erected

Love is ephemeral, yet necessary
How would the world otherwise
Continue its existence

Love is selfish, yet beautiful
How would humanity otherwise
learn to grow

When love becomes pure, the futility
Of efforts get exposed
Erasing duality, from the heart

Love's Lies -- Mukesh Chhajer

Love teases, to test patience
Surrenders, when least expected
How is one to know though
When the cross-over would occur

Love's Lies -- Mukesh Chhajer

Before love, I was empty
After love, I am empty
In between, I have no memory

Even mind gets dissolved
For that brief moment

Love's Lies -- Mukesh Chhajer

Love is not alone
Love does not need company
Love is, and that is how
It would like to be

Love's Lies -- Mukesh Chhajer

Love does not demand, you must be mine
Love does not give, what is unhealthy and harmful
Love does not assert, I am always right
Love merely proposes, I am ever at your service

Love's Lies -- Mukesh Chhajer

Love has many lessons to teach
One thing though it does not
Understand, is bitterness

Love's Lies -- Mukesh Chhajer

Love's latent heat, burns
Not the outer sheath

Love's cooling balm, cleanses
All inner pores

Love's gentle dance, hides
Behind a placid mask

Love's real task, to lead one
To Oneself

Love's Lies -- Mukesh Chhajer

Let love lie low
To recuperate
No one is entitled
To its company, every moment

Love's Lies -- Mukesh Chhajer

Love lags behind, how can
It compete with, the gadgets
That bring, instant gratification

Love's Lies -- Mukesh Chhajer

Love lights a lamp
Are you the oil
That keeps the flame, alive

Love's Lies -- Mukesh Chhajer

Let love linger for a while
Before letting it in
To enjoy it, there must be
A little separation

Love's Lies -- Mukesh Chhajer

Let love flow, like a river
Pollutants only add to, its character

A rose will not be a rose, without its thorns
A lotus will not grow, without mud
Fragrance is a slave, of a decaying flower
Let love be decorated, by a few dark spots

Moon has craters, sun its flares
Stars don't even know, what are they worth
Space wanders alone, without company
Let love fill, the void within

Love's Lies -- Mukesh Chhajer

When love rolled its eyes
Everything got suffused with its light
Gold and diamond shine, only
In empty spaces

Love's Lies -- Mukesh Chhajer

Love is a suffering that
Few are privileged to endure
And even fewer are strong enough
To emerge from it, purified to the core

Love's Lies -- Mukesh Chhajer

In love, there is no laughter or tears
Just a serene smile

Love's Lies -- Mukesh Chhajer

Let love run wild
If the walls crumble down
If the barn burns down
You will receive, the protection of the sky

Love's Lies -- Mukesh Chhajer

Only love knows, pain and pleasure are fake
Only love knows, joy and sorrow are superficial
Only love knows, yours and mine is insane
Only love knows, duality is an illusion

Love's Lies -- Mukesh Chhajer

Love is fire, are you
Gold or dry grass
Think carefully before you
Step in the pit

Love is wind, are you
A banyan tree or a loose leaf
Think carefully before you
Step in its path

Love is water, are you
The ocean or a tiny pond
Think carefully before you
Invite the rain

Love's Lies -- Mukesh Chhajer

Love's cries, reverberate in the sky
Calm, pleasant, joyous
Pain and sorrow, even if present
Enhance the pleasure, many-fold

Love's Lies -- Mukesh Chhajer

When in love, time is a slave
When by the side of the beloved
When in love, time is a tyrant
When beloved is far away

Love and time, the two pillars
Of life don't understand
How to be temperate

Love's Lies -- Mukesh Chhajer

Never will I be, your slave
Never will I be, your master
Never will I be, your friend
Beloved and I are, forever one

When the forces of the world are at play
Distances must maintain their existence
When duality of nature raises head
How will one arrive, completely naked

When give-and-take is constantly balanced
Conflicts become essential
When mind races ahead of the heart
How can one become, completely null

All relations I live with are myth
Can a corner be your friend in a room, non-existent
Sun is alone, stars exist in isolation
Time, for them, is a measure, inconsequential

Love's Lies -- Mukesh Chhajer

Love has lost its way

A river lost in mid-stream
A ray lost in empty space
A breath lost in lungs
A death, unaware of itself

Will it ever reach its destination

Love's Lies -- Mukesh Chhajer

In love, don't surrender
In love, don't conquer
In love, dissolve
Like sugar in water

Love's Lies -- Mukesh Chhajer

Let love not be ruined
By demands, unreasonable

Let love not be ruined
By attention, excessive

Let love not be ruined
By truth, brutal

Let love not be ruined
By lies, too sweet

Love's Lies -- Mukesh Chhajer

Love does not lie, but cheats
Love does not die, but retreats
Love does not fight, but kills
Love does not take, but robs

Without rules, love thrives
With rules, it does not exist

Love's Lies -- Mukesh Chhajer

Love that does not touch
The dirt
Is not true or honest

Love that does not cause
Any hurt
Is superficial

Love that promises
Only celebrations
Is empty and hollow

Love that demands
Incessantly
Quickly, falls apart

Love's Lies -- Mukesh Chhajer

How can you and I be separate
When your heart beats, in my chest

How can you and I be distant
When your presence, I feel everywhere

How can you and I be strangers
When your thought guides, my every action

How can you and I be not one
When without you, I don't exist

Love's Lies -- Mukesh Chhajer

No potion is strong enough
To cast away the spell that
Weaves itself into the heart
Uninvited

Love's Lies -- Mukesh Chhajer

A rose amongst thorns
A lotus amidst mud
An oasis in a desert
Love and its entourage

Love's Lies -- Mukesh Chhajer

Love is not a flower
Neither a river, nor an ocean

Love is a little thorn
That tucks at your heart

Until you have accepted
The inevitable

Love's Lies -- Mukesh Chhajer

Love is a death, of selfishness
Love is a defeat, of greed
Love is a victory, over passions
Love is a celebration, of the spirit

About Author

Mukesh Chhajer lives in Danville VA where he teaches math and physics. Writing poetry is his hobby. He has previously published six books: four collections of poetry including one in Hindi, a biography of Mahaveer Swami in verse and one book of essays on Jainism.

www.ingramcontent.com/pod-product-compliance
Lightning Source LLC
Chambersburg PA
CBHW061332040426
42444CB00011B/2875